# Duets from Broadway

INTER

MW00783770

## AN COATES — POPULAR PIANO LIBRARY

Since 1976, Dan Coates has arranged thousands of popular music titles. Composers and artists such as John Williams, Burt Bacharach, and Elton John have expressed total confidence in Dan's ability to create outstanding piano arrangements that retain the essence of the original music. He has arranged everything from movie, television, and Broadway themes to chart-topping pop and rock titles. In addition to creating piano arrangements for players of all levels, Dan also composes original music for student pianists.

The duets in this series capture a variety of styles and provide valuable experiences in developing listening skills, technique, and musicianship. They are arranged for one piano, four hands, with the *primo* and *secondo* parts on separate, facing pages. Measure numbers are provided for easy reference, while suggestions for fingering and dynamics help prepare students for rehearsals and performances. These pieces are excellent crowd-pleasers that are perfect for recitals, encores, piano ensemble classes—or just plain fun.

## CONTENTS

| SONG | SHOW | PAGE |
|------|------|------|
| And All That Jazz | *Chicago* | 2 |
| Anything Goes | *Anything Goes* | 12 |
| Camelot | *Camelot* | 18 |
| Don't Rain on My Parade | *Funny Girl* | 28 |
| I Have a Dream | *Mamma Mia!* | 36 |
| Ragtime | *Ragtime* | 42 |
| Supercalifragilisticexpialidocious | Walt Disney's *Mary Poppins* | 48 |
| Together Wherever We Go | *Gypsy* | 56 |

Produced by
Alfred Music Publishing Co., Inc.
P.O. Box 10003
Van Nuys, CA 91410-0003
alfred.com

Printed in USA.

ISBN-10: 0-7390-9210-3
ISBN-13: 978-0-7390-9210-1

# And All That Jazz

(from *Chicago*)

SECONDO

Lyrics by FRED EBB
Music by JOHN KANDER
Arranged by Dan Coates

Moderately, with a deliberate beat

# And All That Jazz

### (from *Chicago*)

**PRIMO**

Lyrics by FRED EBB
Music by JOHN KANDER
Arranged by Dan Coates

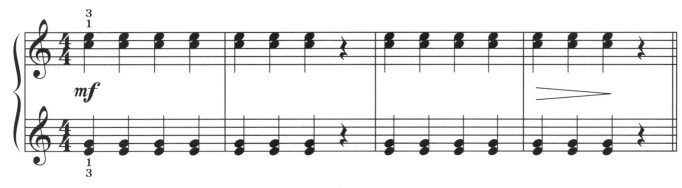

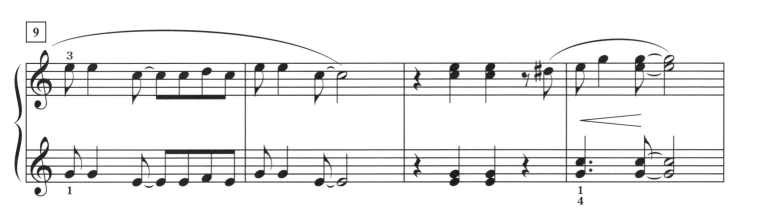

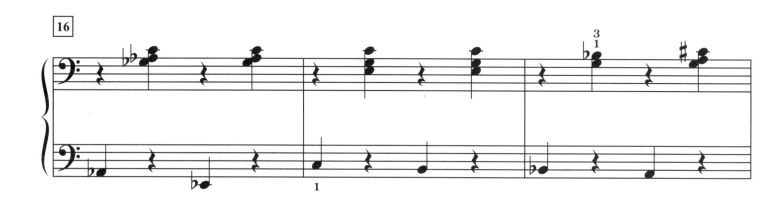

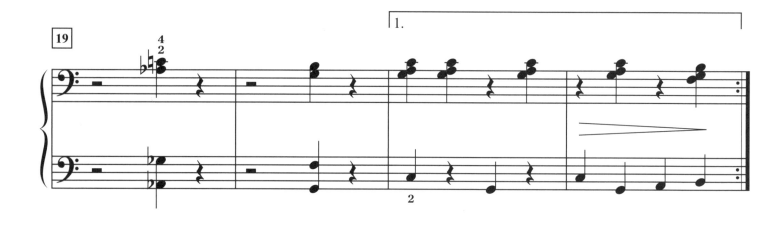

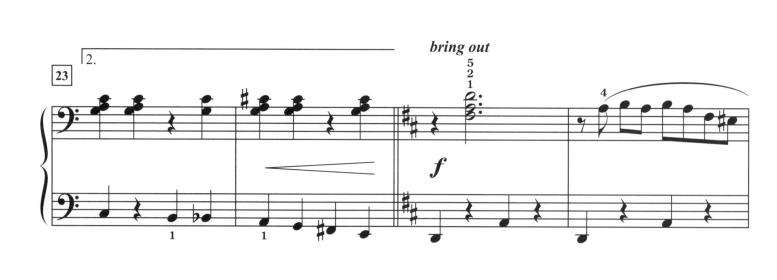

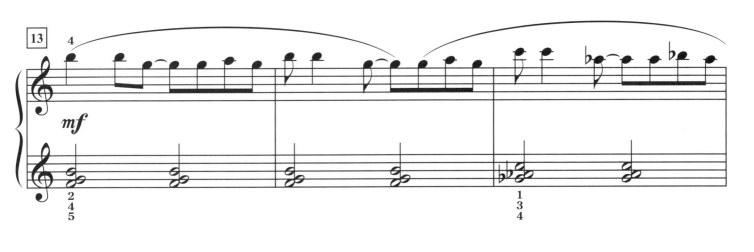

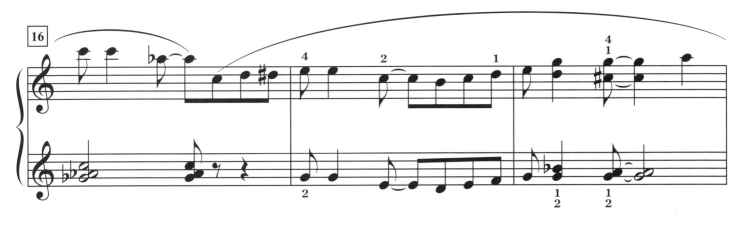

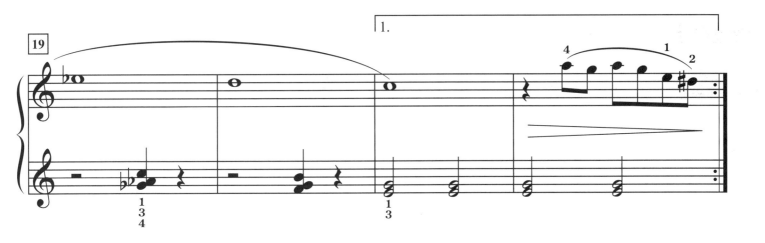

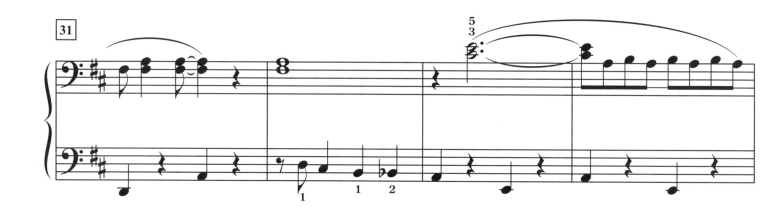

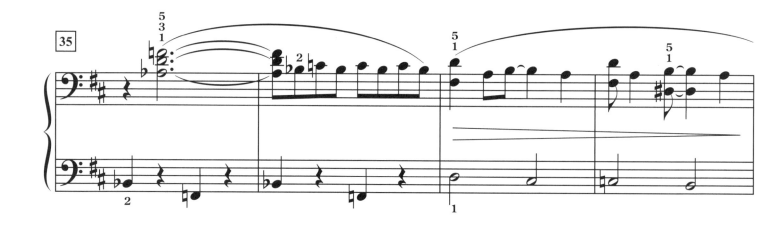

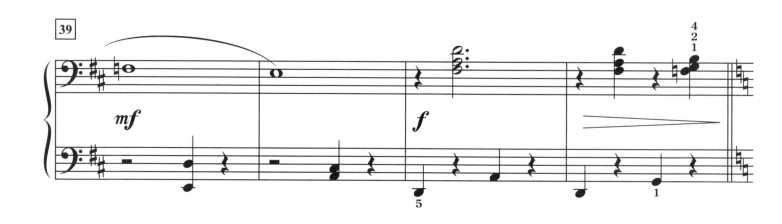

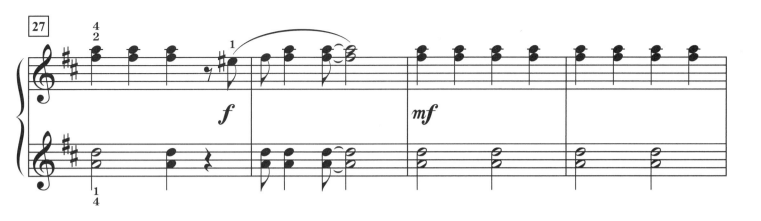

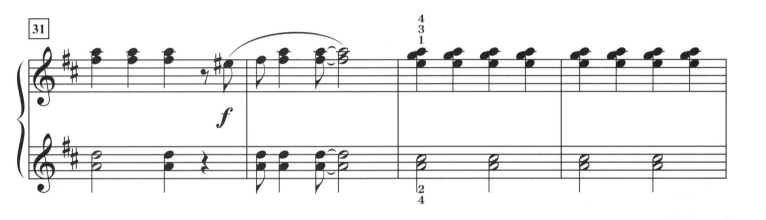

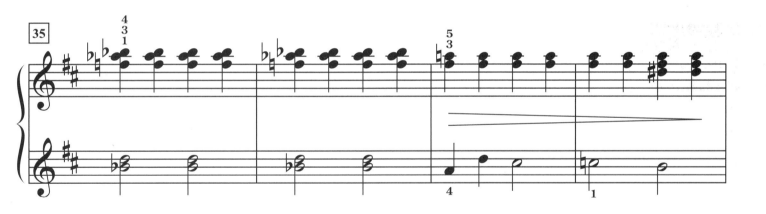

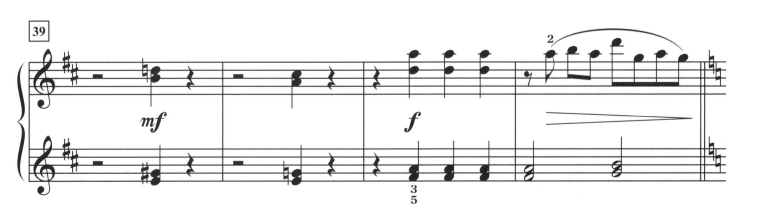

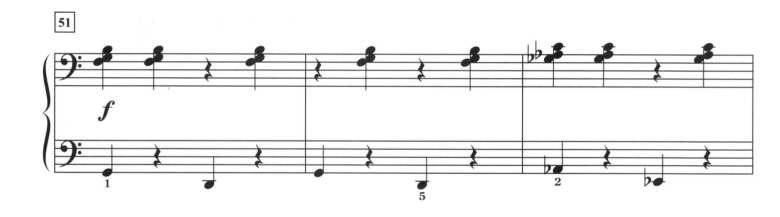

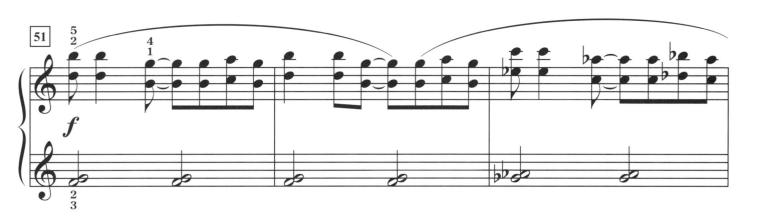

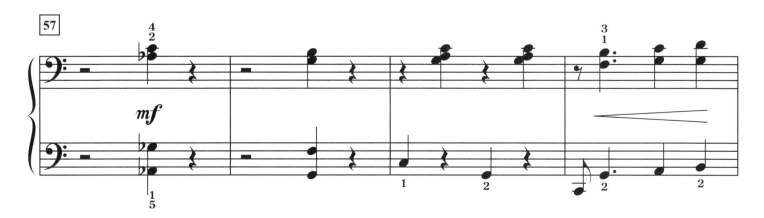

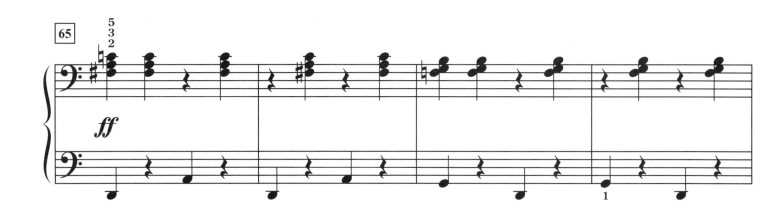

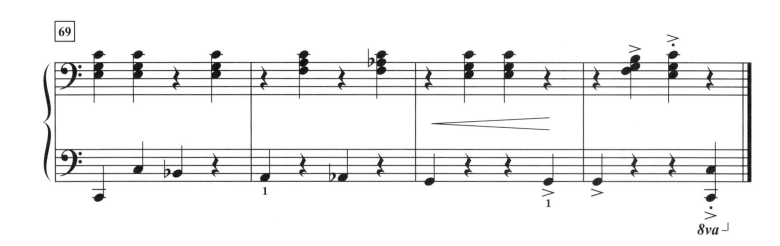

*8va*

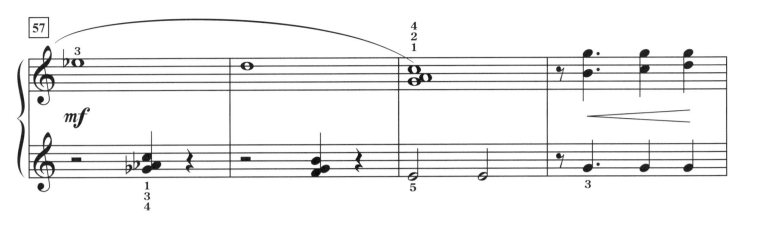

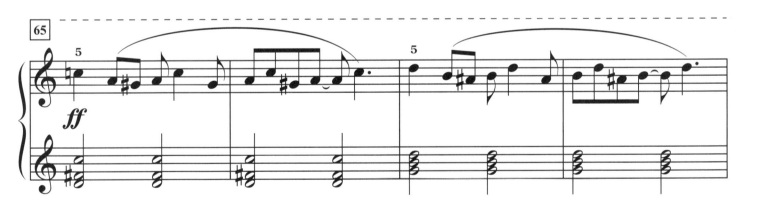

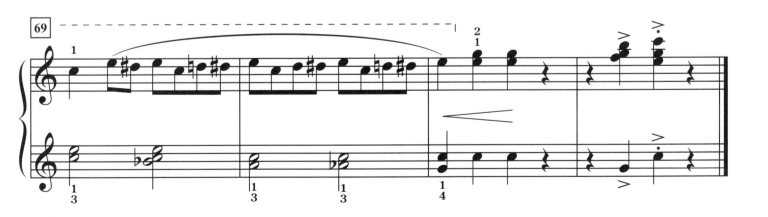

# Anything Goes

(from *Anything Goes*)

**SECONDO**

Words and Music by COLE PORTER
Arranged by Dan Coates

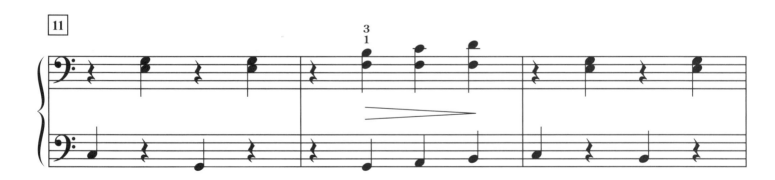

# Anything Goes

## (from *Anything Goes*)

**PRIMO**

Words and Music by COLE PORTER
Arranged by Dan Coates

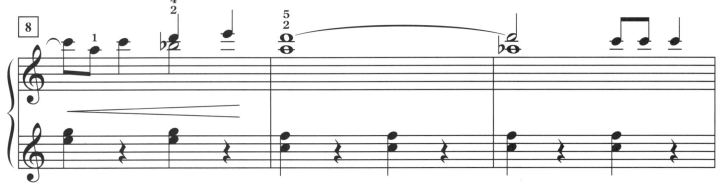

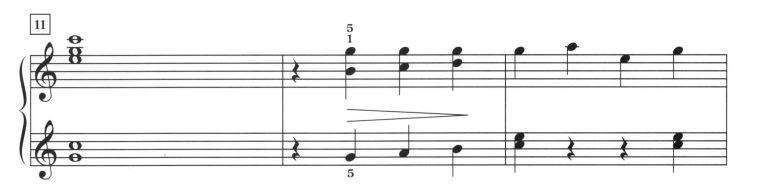

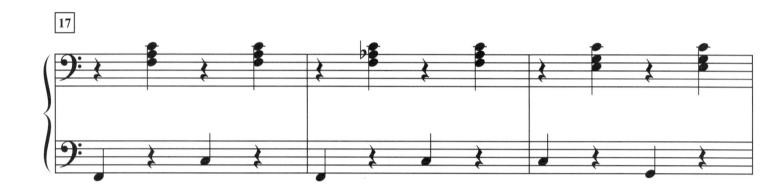

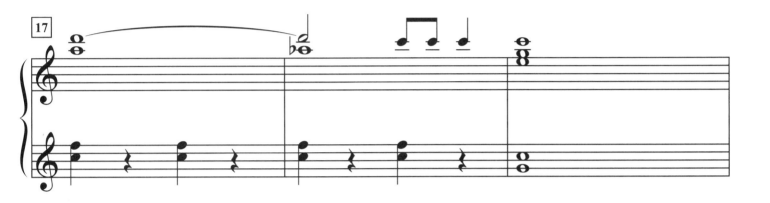

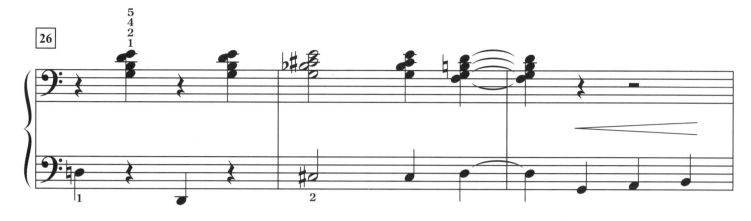

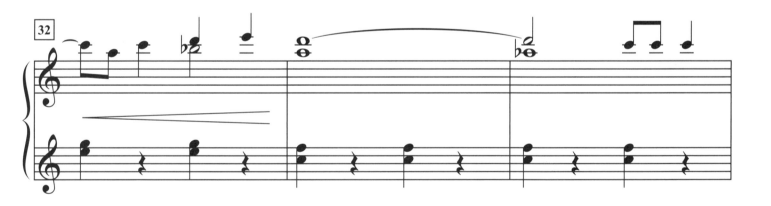

# Camelot
## (from *Camelot*)

### SECONDO

Words by ALAN JAY LERNER
Music by FREDERICK LOEWE
Arranged by Dan Coates

# Camelot

(from *Camelot*)

## PRIMO

Words by ALAN JAY LERNER
Music by FREDERICK LOEWE
Arranged by Dan Coates

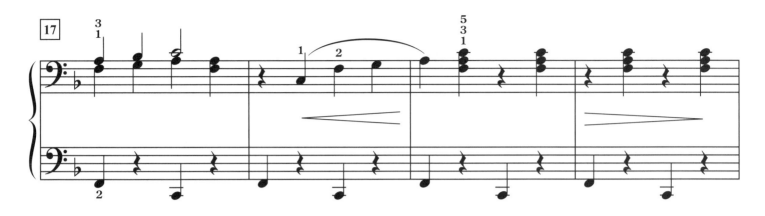

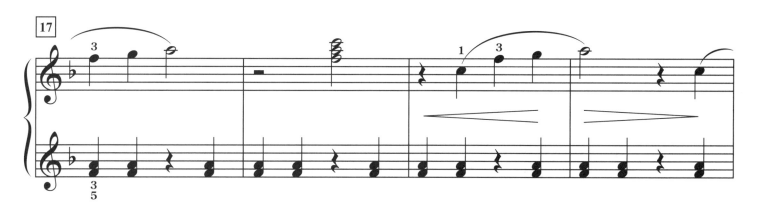

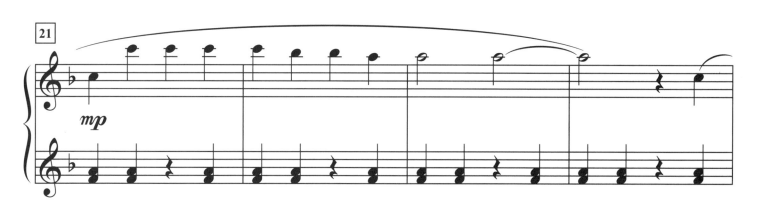

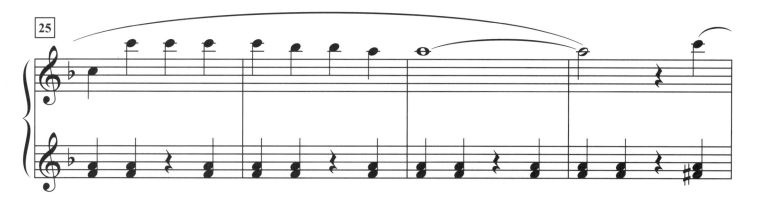

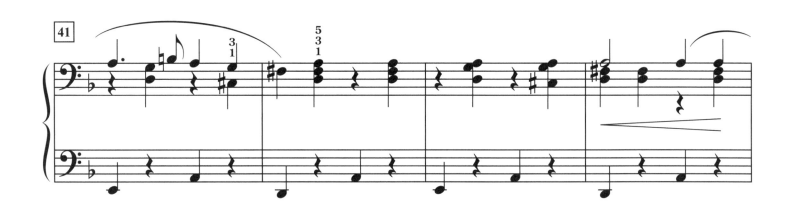

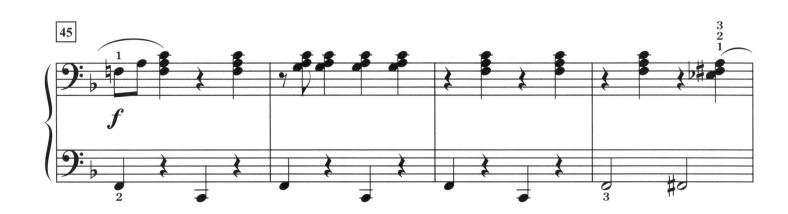

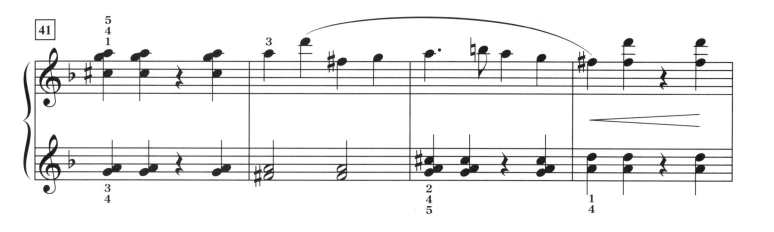

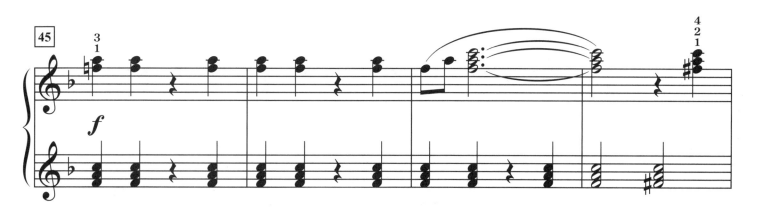

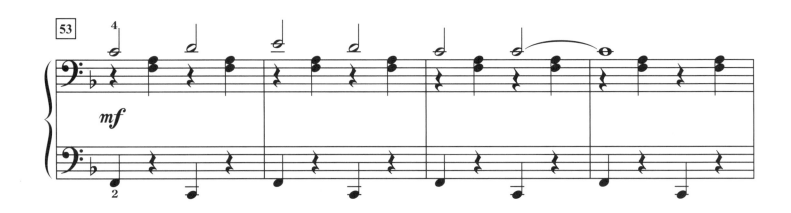

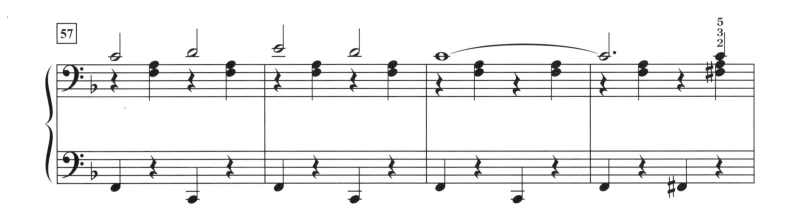

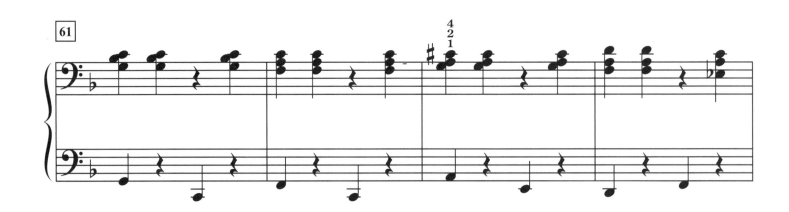

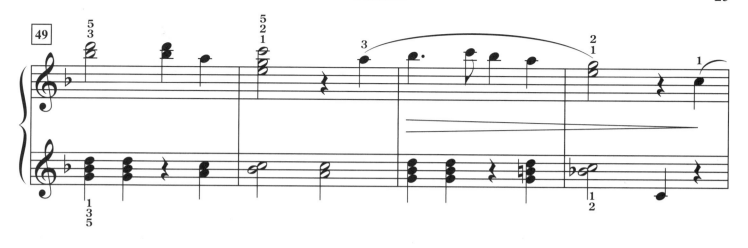

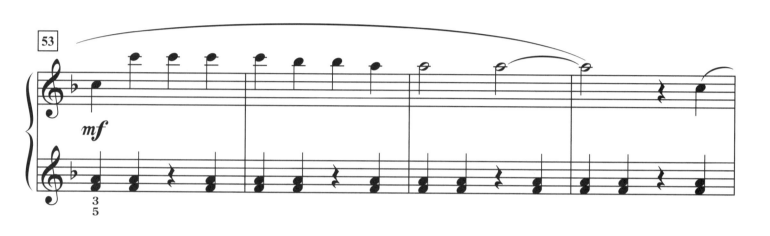

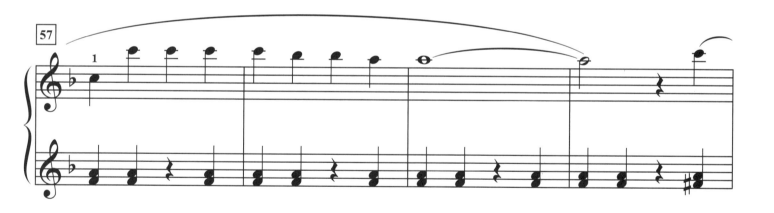

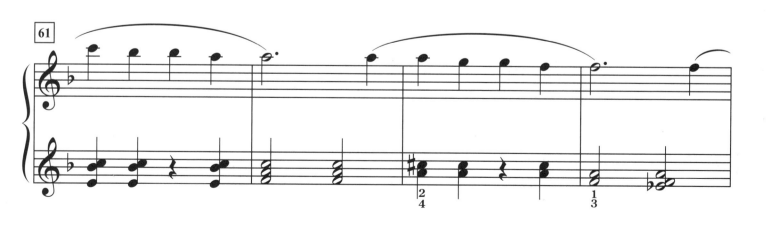

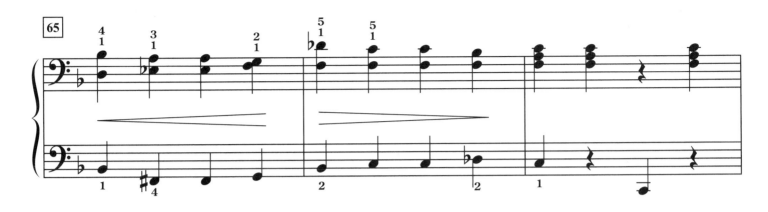

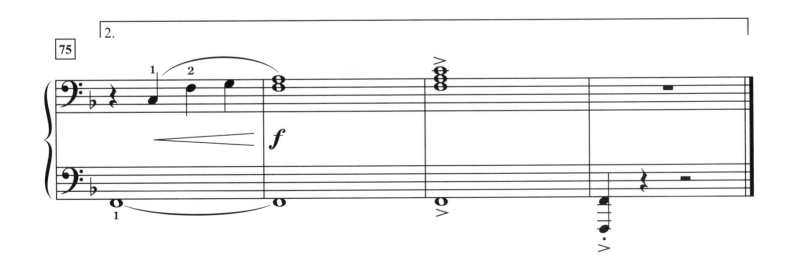

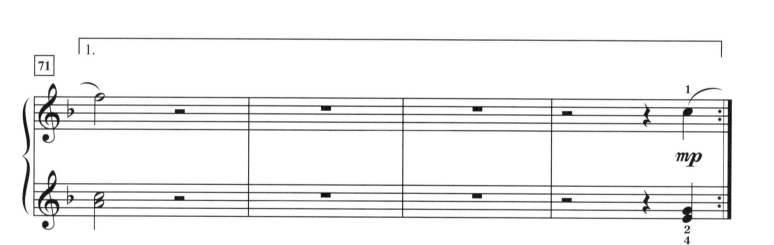

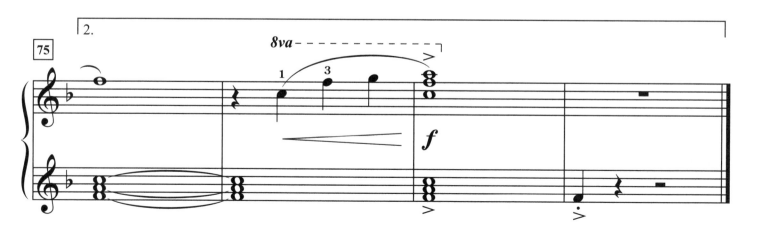

# Don't Rain on My Parade

(from *Funny Girl*)

SECONDO

Words by BOB MERRILL
Music by JULE STYNE
Arranged by Dan Coates

**Brightly, with a steady beat**

# Don't Rain on My Parade

(from *Funny Girl*)

**PRIMO**

Words by BOB MERRILL
Music by JULE STYNE
Arranged by Dan Coates

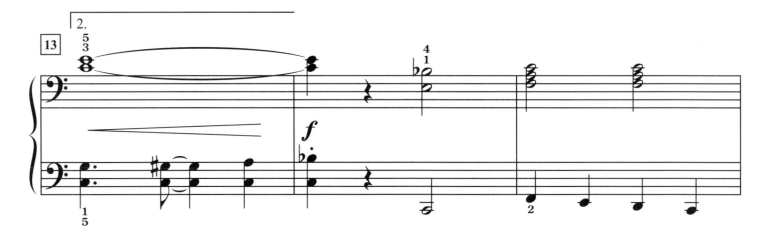

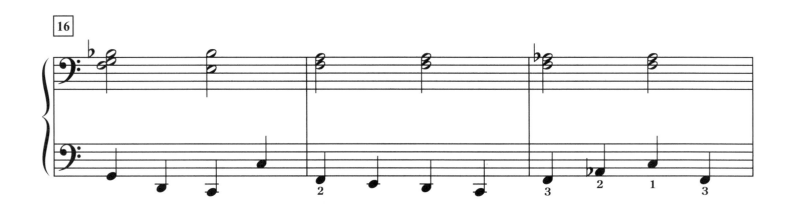

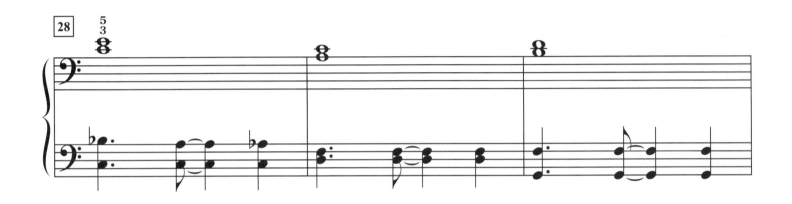

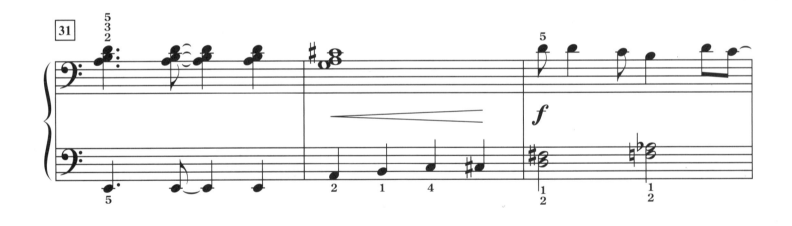

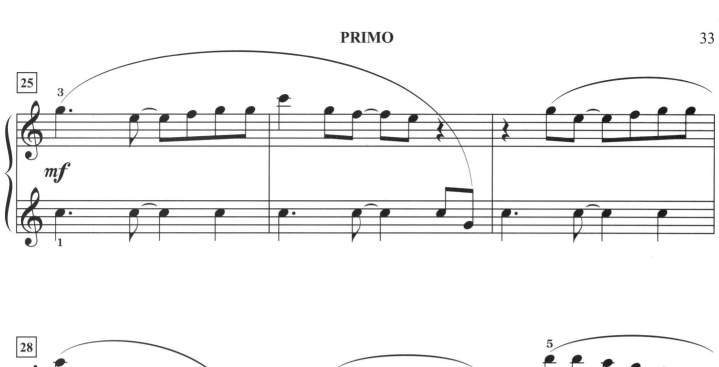

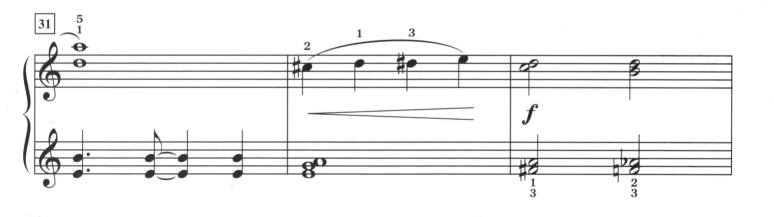

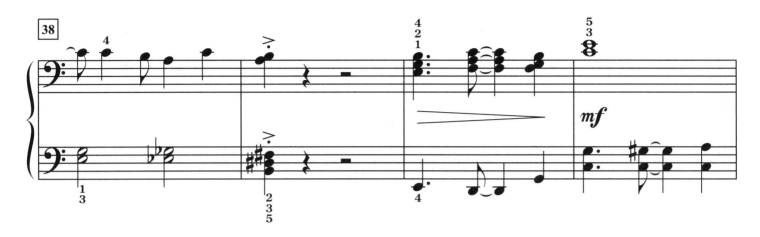

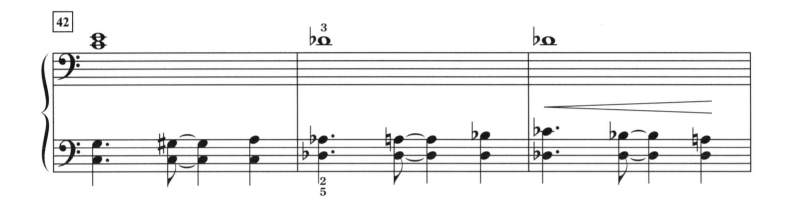

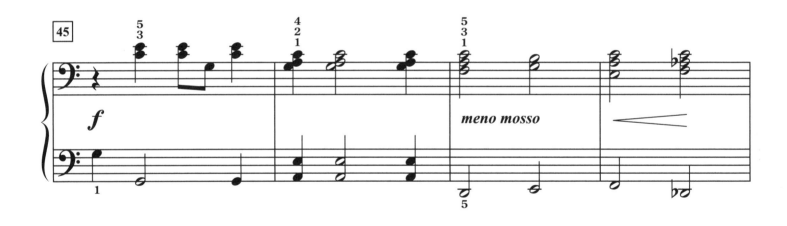

# I Have a Dream

## (from *Mamma Mia!*)

### SECONDO

Words and Music by
BENNY ANDERSSON and BJORN ULVAEUS
Arranged by Dan Coates

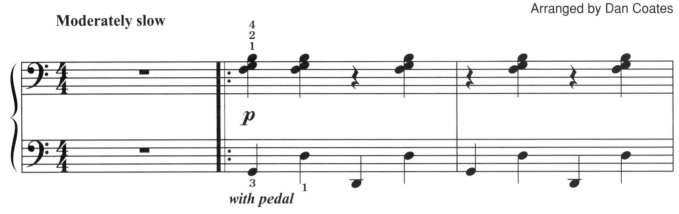

# I Have a Dream

(from *Mamma Mia!*)

**PRIMO**

Words and Music by
BENNY ANDERSSON and BJORN ULVAEUS
Arranged by Dan Coates

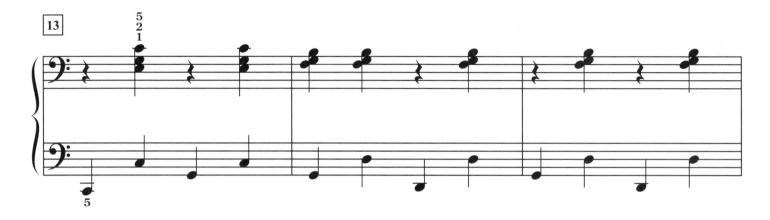

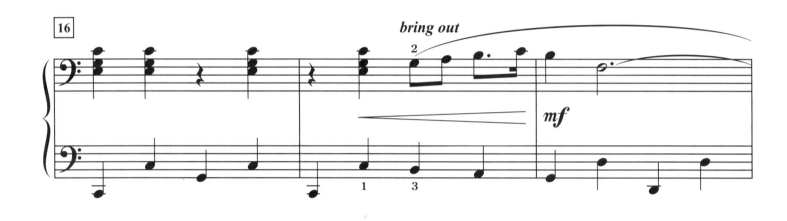

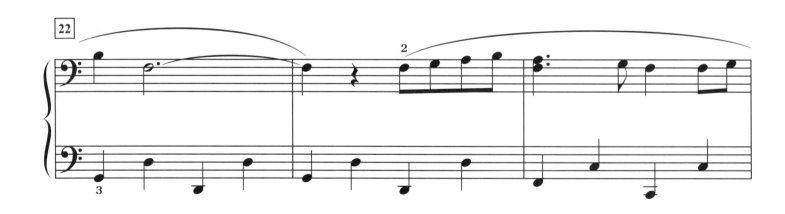

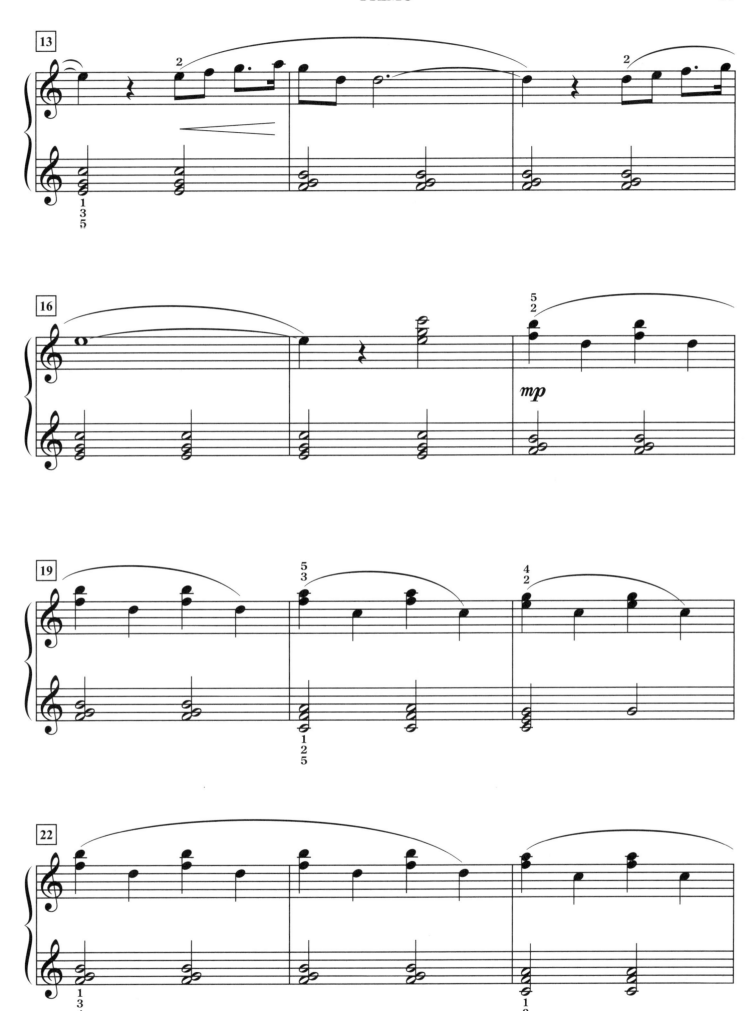

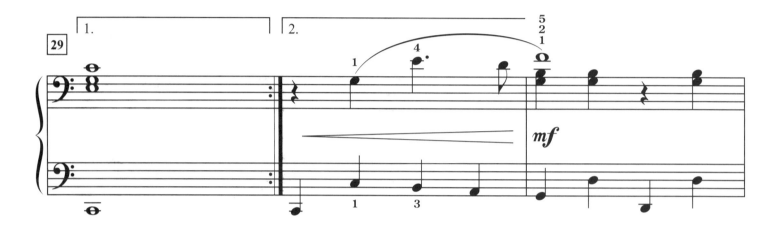

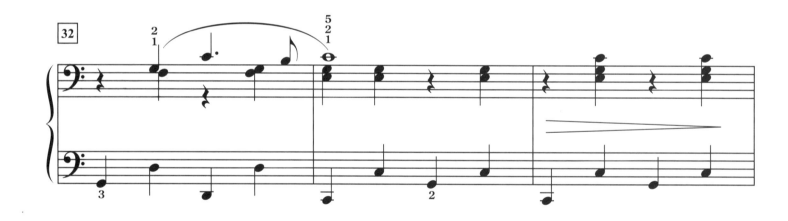

# Ragtime

(from *Ragtime*)

### SECONDO

Lyrics by LYNN AHRENS
Music by STEPHEN FLAHERTY
Arranged by Dan Coates

**Moderato (not too quickly)**

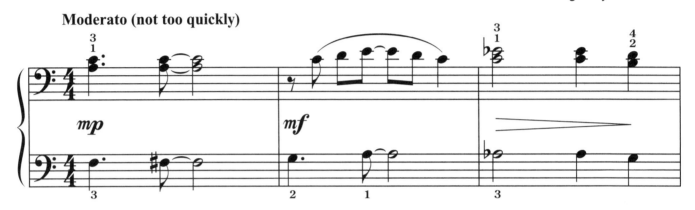

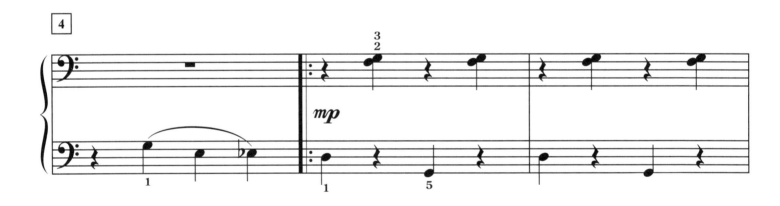

# Ragtime
(from *Ragtime*)

**PRIMO**

Lyrics by LYNN AHRENS
Music by STEPHEN FLAHERTY
Arranged by Dan Coates

**Moderato (Not too quickly)**

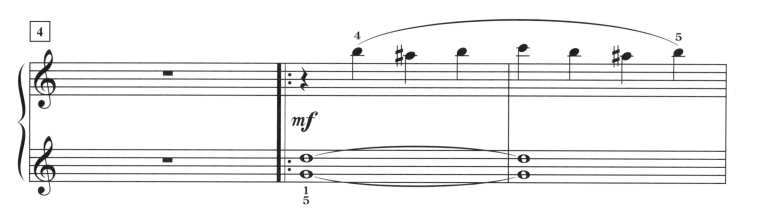

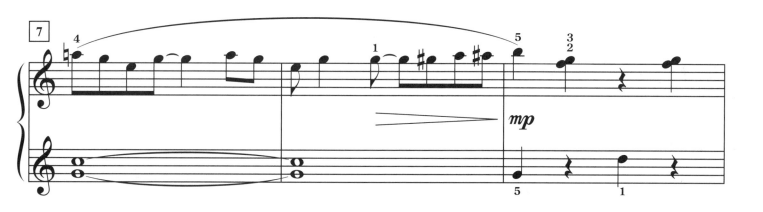

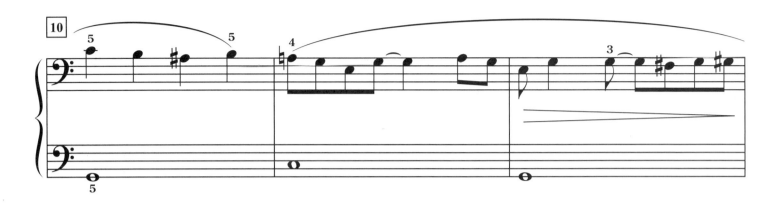

*cresc. poco a poco*

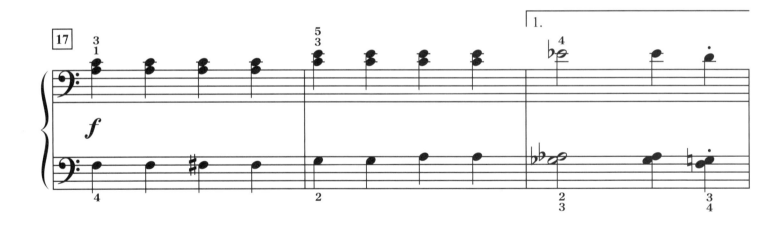

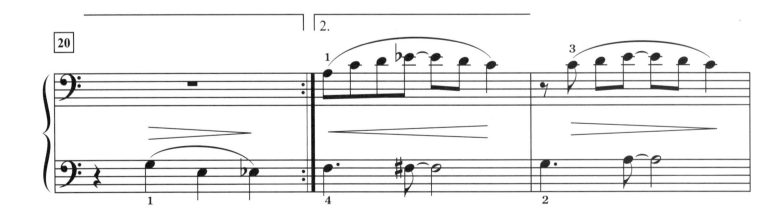

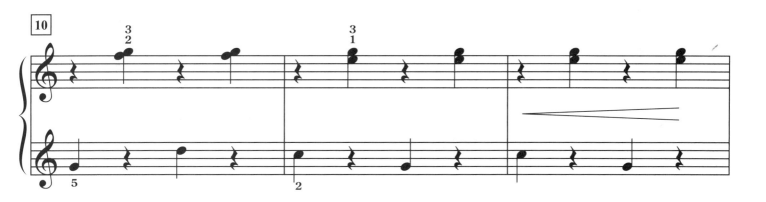

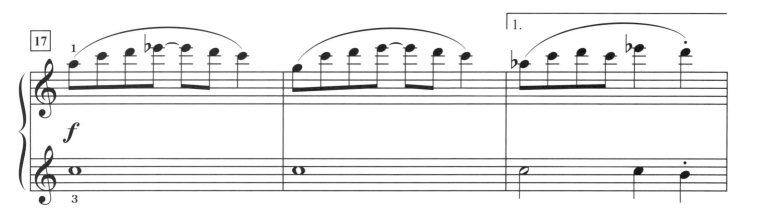

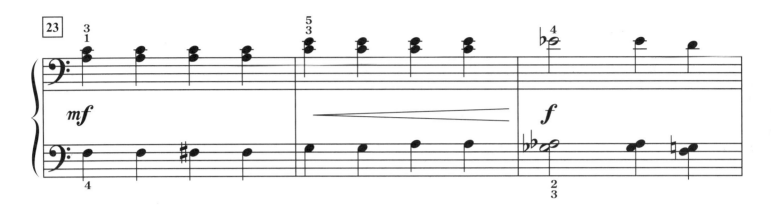

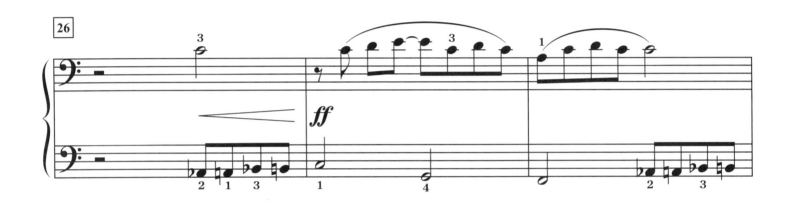

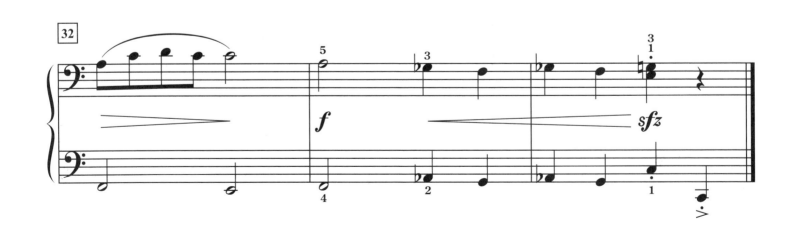

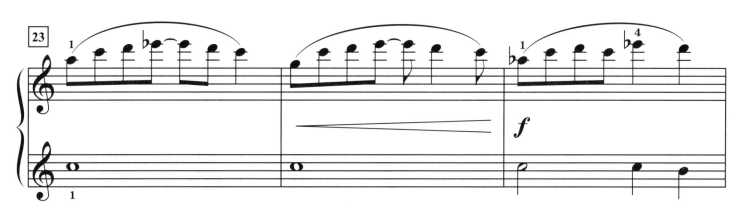

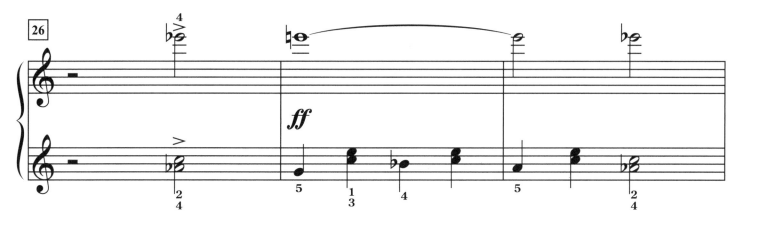

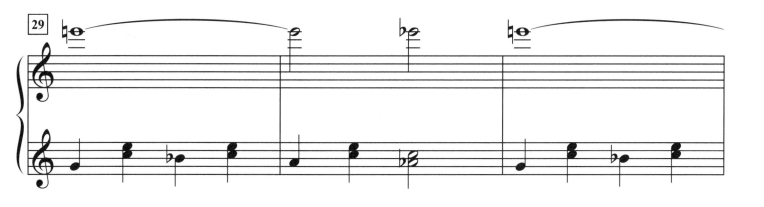

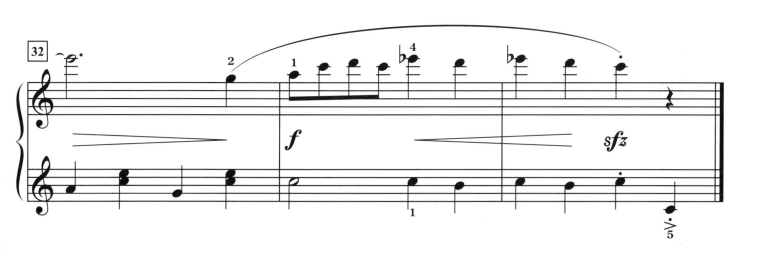

# Supercalifragilisticexpialidocious

(from Walt Disney's *Mary Poppins*)

**SECONDO**

Words and Music by
RICHARD M. SHERMAN and ROBERT B. SHERMAN
Arranged by Dan Coates

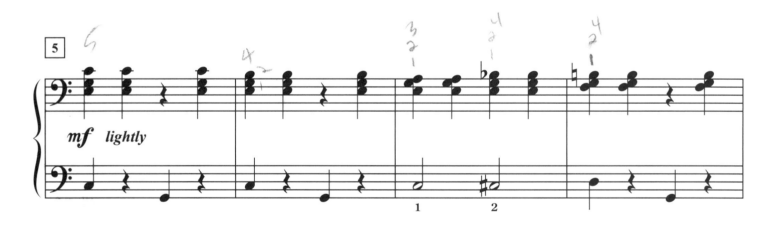

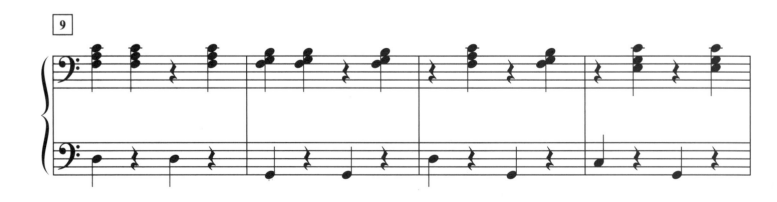

# Supercalifragilisticexpialidocious

(from Walt Disney's *Mary Poppins*)

**PRIMO**

Words and Music by
RICHARD M. SHERMAN and ROBERT B. SHERMAN
Arranged by Dan Coates

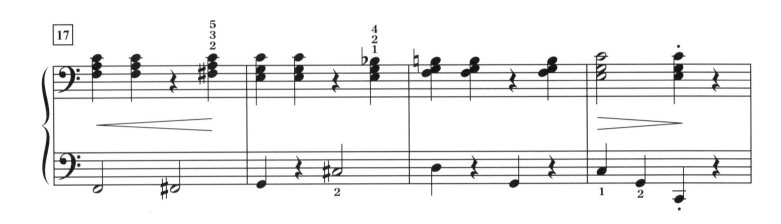

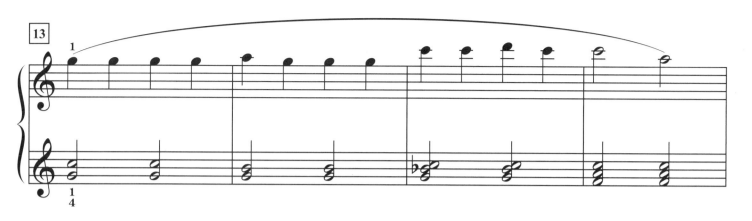

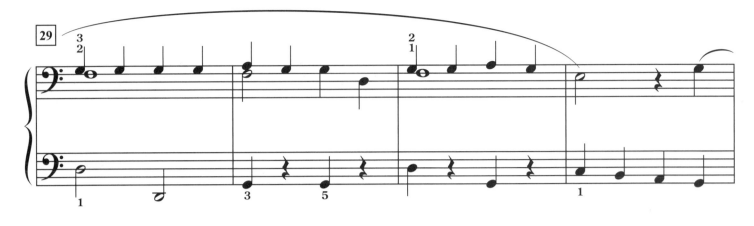

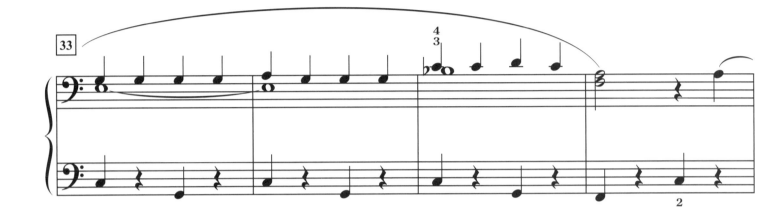

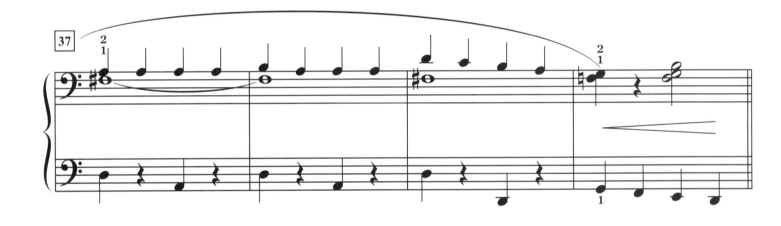

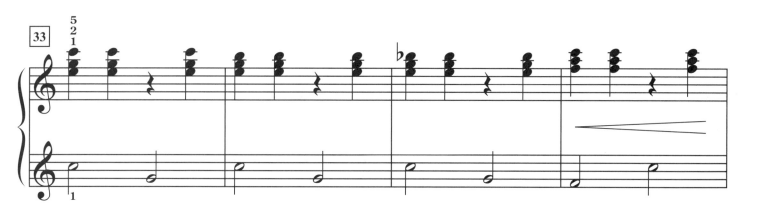

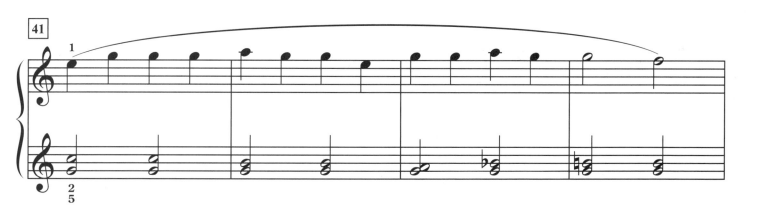

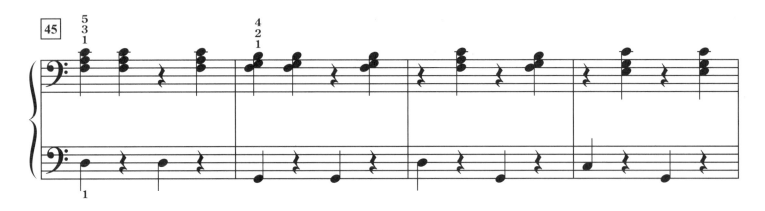

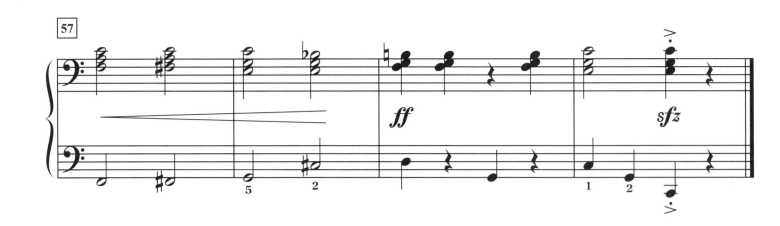

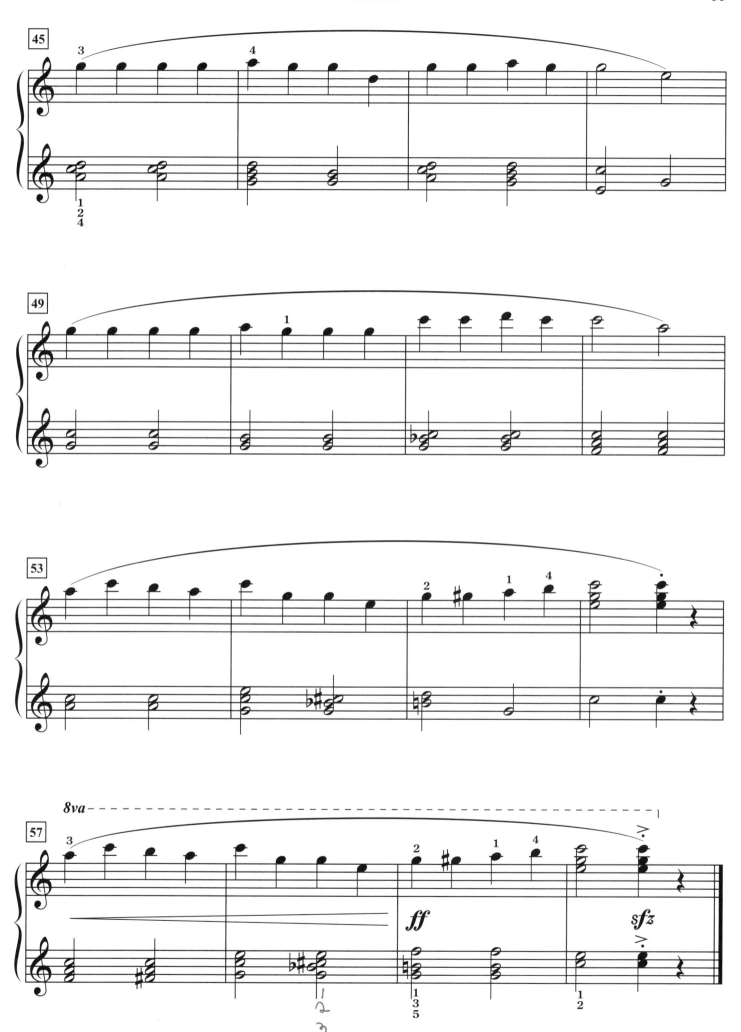

# Together Wherever We Go

(from *Gypsy*)

**SECONDO**

Lyrics by STEPHEN SONDHEIM
Music by JULE STYNE
Arranged by Dan Coates

**Brightly, in two**

# Together Wherever We Go

## (from *Gypsy*)

### PRIMO

Lyrics by STEPHEN SONDHEIM
Music by JULE STYNE
Arranged by Dan Coates

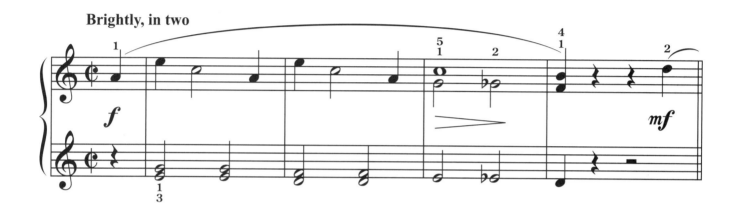

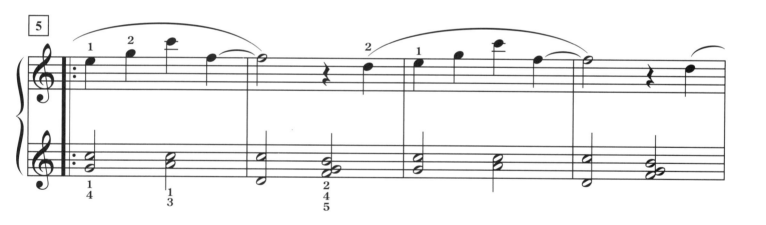

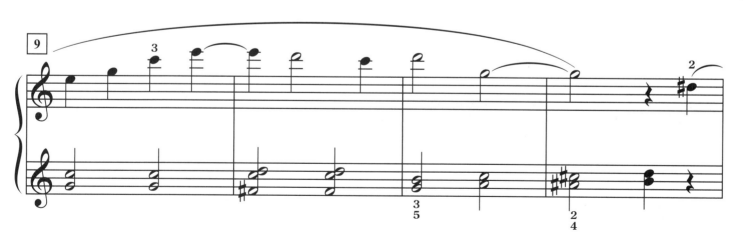

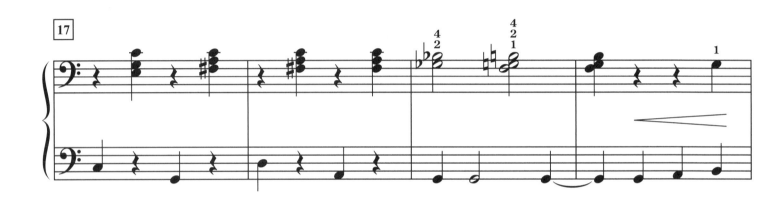

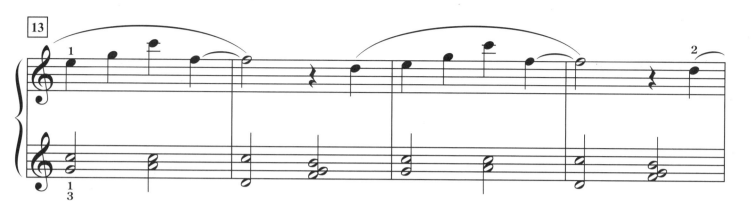

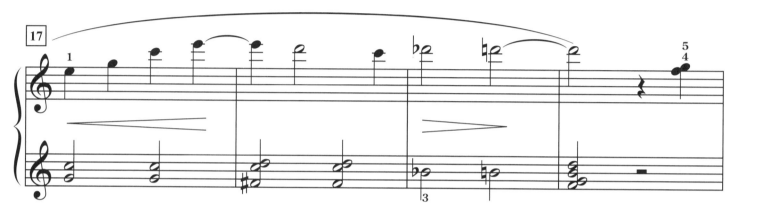

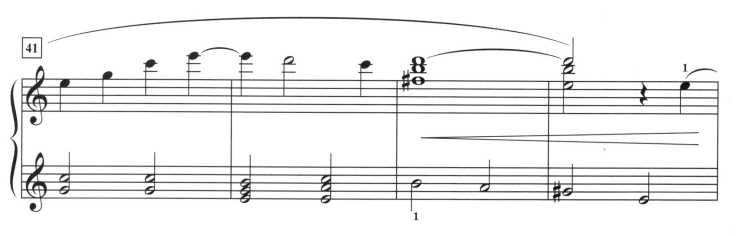

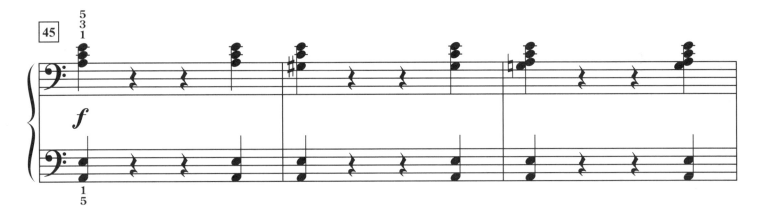

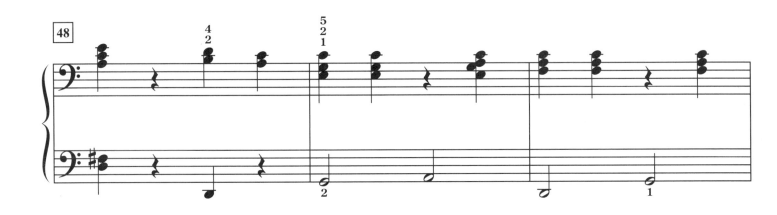